REFLECTIONS OF GRACE

Reflections of Grace

CYNTHIA GREELY

PURELILLY PRESS

ISBN: 978-1-965050-04-0

Published by Purelilly Press Publishing
Huntsville, Texas

First Printing, 2025

CONTENTS

DEDICATION

This book is devoted and dedicated to:

My mother:

You have been my rock, my confidence, and my greatest cheerleader. From the earliest days of my life, you have nurtured and guided me with unconditional love and unwavering devotion. Your prayers, your wisdom, and your encouragement have shaped me into the person I am today. Your faithfulness and strength inspire me to walk boldly in the path you have set before me, knowing that your love will always be my guiding light.

Proverbs 31:28-29

Her children arise and call her blessed; her husband also and he praises her; Many women do noble things, but you surpass them all.

My son:

To my beloved son, who has been my greatest inspiration and source of strength throughout our seven-day journey.

As a single mom who faced many challenges and uncertainties, your unwavering love and resilience lifted my spirits and gave me the courage to press on. You have taught me the true meaning of unconditional love, forgiveness, and perseverance.

Psalm 127:3
Children are a heritage from the Lord, offspring a reward from him.

My husband:

To my beloved husband, you are my partner, my best friend, and my greatest blessing. Your love, your patience, and your unwavering support have sustained me through the highs and the lows of life's journey. In moments when doubts crept in, and others questioned my abilities, your unwavering faith in me never changed. Your belief in my potential and your encouragement to pursue it greatly propelled me forward, even when the path seemed uncertain. I'm grateful that God is guiding us to walk hand in hand together along this journey.

Ecclesiastes 4:9-10

Two are better than one, because they have a good return for their labor; If either of them falls down, one can help the other up. But pity anyone who falls and has no one to help them up.

INTRODUCTION

During a time when I navigated the challenges of being a single mother, I discovered the profound impact of daily reflection and prayer on my spiritual well-being. I made a simple decision: take seven days and focus on my Heavenly Father. That simple decision became a turning point in my life, deepening my connection with God and transforming my walk of faith.

May Reflections of Grace be a source of encouragement and inspiration, leading you to a deeper understanding of God's love and grace in your life.

~ 1 ~

DAY ONE

EMBRACING GRATITUDE

Psalm 107:1

Give thanks to the Lord, for he is good; his love endures forever.

During my journey, I encountered many challenges as a single mother. There were moments when I felt overwhelmed and alone, but, through it all, God never left me. His presence was my constant source of strength and comfort, and for that, I am truly grateful.

Financial Pressure

Single parents often bear the full weight of providing for their children, which can bring stress and uncertainty.

Feelings of Isolation

Without a partner to share responsibilities, single parents may feel isolated and overwhelmed by the daily demands.

Balance

Single parents often juggle full-time jobs and parent duties, which can lead to feelings of guilt or a sense of not having enough time for their children.

Worry

Worrying about the future, concerns about providing a stable future, and raising their children alone can weigh heavily on single parents' minds. Going through a divorce or separation or difficult breakup, especially when it involves parenting, can bring unique pain and struggles.

There's Always Hope

Despite the heavy responsibilities of a single parent, I held on to my faith and refused to give up, trusting that God would provide the strength I needed each day. Even when I didn't have all the answers, I leaned on God, trusting His plan and wisdom would fill the gaps and lead me through every challenge. God helped me through the difficult times, giving me strength when I felt weak and guiding me when I couldn't see the future. I didn't give up because I knew my dreams and prayers would be answered in God's timing.

Reflect

Write down a time when you felt God's presence and provision in your life, even under challenging circumstances. How did His faithfulness impact your perspective and attitude?

_____

_____

_____

_____

_____

_____

_____

_____

_____

_____

~ 2 ~

DAY TWO

MINDFULLNESS

Psalm 46: 10

He says, "Be still and know that I am God: I will be exalted among the nations, I will be exalted in the earth."

Cultivating Mindfulness

During my journey, I struggled to find time to be still in God's presence. It wasn't until I made a conscious effort to prioritize moments of quiet reflection each day that I began to experience a deeper sense of peace and connection with God. Through disciplined practice, I learned to tune out the noise of the world and focus my attention on God's voice speaking to me.

What challenges do you face in setting a quiet time for prayer and reflection?

How can you overcome those challenges and cultivate a deeper sense of mindfulness in your daily walk? During my time as a single parent, I developed simple but powerful habits to stay grounded in God's peace. Each morning, I would begin with gratitude and a prayer for strength, reminding myself that God was with me. Through my lunch break, I found quiet moments to reflect, release my worries, and center my thoughts. In the evening, I would reflect on the day, surrender any burdens to God, and close with His Word, trusting that He would give me rest. These small moments of stillness helped me navigate the challenges of single parenting and kept me connected to God's presence.

Take a moment to commit to intentionally being still before God each day. Write down what you hear and experience during your time with God each day. Start today!

_____

_____

_____

_____

_____

_____

_____

_____

_____

~ 3 ~

DAY THREE

JOURNEY TO FORGIVENESS

Ephesians 4:32

*Be kind and compassionate to one another, forgiving each
other, just as Christ God forgives you.*

During my journey, I faced numerous hurts and disap-
pointments at the hands of others. The weight of
bitterness and resentment threatened to consume me,
and forgiveness seemed like an impossible feat! Yet,
through God's grace and mercy, I found strength to release the hurt and anger that had been weighing me
down. It was a process that required time, prayer, and a
willingness to let go of the past, but in the end, it brought

me freedom! God's healing touch transformed my heart and allowed me to move forward with hope and grace.

Reflect on any past hurts or grievances you're holding on to and consider the possibility of extending forgiveness to those who have wronged you. How might the act of forgiveness bring healing and freedom to your life? Please take a moment to write a letter of forgiveness to someone who has hurt you, releasing them from the debt you feel they owe you.

Dear............

_____

_____

_____

_____

_____

_____

_____

_____

_____

_____

_____

_____

_____

_____

_____

_____

_____

~ 4 ~

DAY FOUR

FINDING STRENGTH IN ADVERSITY

Isaiah 41:10

So do not fear, for I am with you; do not be dismayed, for I am your God. I will strengthen you and help you; I will uphold you with my righteous right hand.

During my journey, I encountered numerous obstacles and trials that seemed intent on stopping God's plan for my life. There were moments when I felt overwhelmed and discouraged, and it seemed like the odds were stacked against me.

There were times when I feared I wouldn't have enough money to cover doctor bills, daycare, groceries, etc., but God always provided. His provision came just in time, meeting our needs in ways I could never have anticipated. God exceeded my expectations, providing more than I could ever imagine in ways that reminded me of His faithfulness and love.

Through God's grace and power, I found the strength to persevere! Despite the attempts to thwart his plans, God's purpose prevailed, and I emerged from each trial stronger and more resilient than before. I learned I could rely on God's faithfulness and strength to carry me through.

Reflect

Think about a time when you faced a significant obstacle or trial that threatened to derail God's plan for your life. How did you find strength and courage amid adversity? Please take a moment to write it down. Reflect and express gratitude for God's faithfulness and provision during your time of trial.

_____

_____

_____

_____

_____

_____

_____

_____

_____

_____

~ 5 ~

DAY FIVE

TRUSTING GOD'S PLAN

Jeremiah 29:11

"For I know the plans I have for you," declares the Lord, "plans to prosper you and not to harm you, plans to give you hope and a future."

During my journey, there were moments when I couldn't make sense of God's plan for my life. His leading seemed unclear, and I questioned whether I was on the right path. Yet, as I continued to trust in his guidance and surrender my plan to his will, I began to see his hand at work in ways I never imagined. What initially seemed like detours and setbacks was part of God's perfect plan to lead me to where he wanted me to be. Looking back, I can see how every step, every obstacle, and every blessing lined up according to his purpose, bringing me to a place of greater fulfillment and joy!

Reflect

Think about a time when you initially didn't understand God's plan but later saw everything align according to his purpose. How did you navigate through the uncertainty? How did you feel when you realized God was with you all along?

_____

_____

_____

_____

_____

_____

_____

_____

_____

_____

_____

_____

_____

_____

_____

_____

_____

_____

~ 6 ~

DAY SIX

RESILIENCE IN FAITH!

Philippians 4:13 (AMP)

I can do all things [which He has called me to do] through Him who strengthens and empowers me [to fulfill His purpose—I am self-sufficient in Christ's sufficiency; I am ready for anything and equal to anything through Him who infuses me with inner strength and confident peace.]

During my journey, I faced numerous trials and setbacks that tested my faith. There were moments when I felt like just giving up. The challenges seemed too great to overcome. Yet, in those moments, God's strength sustained me, and his promises gave me hope through prayer, resilience, and grace. I found the courage to press on, knowing that God was with me every step of the way!

Reflect

Think about a time when your faith was tested, and you had to rely on God's strength to preserve you. How did you experience his presence and provision during this time?

_____

_____

_____

_____

_____

_____

_____

_____

_____

_____

_____

_____

_____

_____

_____

_____

_____

_____

_____

_____

_____

_____

_____

_____

~ 7 ~

DAY SEVEN

SURRENDERING TO GOD'S LOVE

Matthew 22:37

Jesus replied: "'Love the Lord your God with all your heart and with all your soul and with all your mind.'

Day seven holds a special significance for me, as it marks the moment when I experienced a profound shift in my relationship with God. It was a day of surrender. A Day when God called me to lay down my own desires and plans and fully embrace his will for my life. It wasn't an easy decision, but I opened my heart to his love and surrendered to his guidance. I experienced a peace and joy that surpassed all understanding. Falling in love with God became the most important and transformative decision I ever made, shaping every aspect of who I am and how I live!

Reflect

Think about a time in your own journey of surrendering to God's love. How has his love transformed your life? Take a moment to write down your reflections and express gratitude for the gift of love.

_____

_____

_____

_____

_____

_____

_____

_____

_____

_____

_____

_____

_____

_____

_____

_____

_____

_____

CONCLUSION

As we conclude the 7th day of this journey together, I want to leave you with a few words to ponder as you navigate your own seasons of trials and triumphs. Life is a journey filled with highs and lows, joys and sorrows. But through it all, God remains faithful. In the midst of your trials, remember that you are never alone. God is with you, guiding you, strengthening you, and carrying you through every storm. Seven days will be a reminder that no matter what you're going through, there is hope. There is a God who loves you unconditionally and works all things together for your good!

PRAYER FOR SALVATION AND RELATIONSHIP WITH GOD

Heavenly Father,

I come before you humbly acknowledging my need for salvation. I recognize that I am a sinner in need of your forgiveness, and I am grateful for the gift of salvation made possible through your son, Jesus Christ.

Please come into my heart, Lord Jesus, and make me new. Wash away my sins with your precious blood and fill me with your Holy Spirit. Amen!